Words Some of Us Rarely Use

For J & A & K, with love

Words Some of Us Rarely Use

Kelly R. Samuels

Copyright © 2018 Kelly R. Samuels
All Rights Reserved.
Published by Unsolicited Press
Portland, Oregon
www.unsolicitedpress.com
Copyright © 2018 Kelly R. Samuels
All Rights Reserved.

No part of this book may be reproduced or transmitted in any form or by any means without written permission from the publisher or author.

For information, contact the publisher at
info@unsolicitedpress.com
Unsolicited Press Books are distributed to the trade by Ingram.
Printed in the United States of America.
ISBN: 978-1-947021-98-3

Thanks to the following journals for publishing versions of poems in this collection:
After the Pause: "Xerosere"
Burningword: "Asomatous," "Lacuna" & "Ort"
Salt Hill: "Quader," "Rimous" & "Yare"
Third Wednesday: "Wanchancy"
The Citron Review: "Petrichor"
Soft Cartel: "Fantod" "Katzenjammer" & "Somaticize"

word

[wurd]

noun

1. a unit of language, consisting of one or more spoken sounds or their written representation, that functions as a principal carrier of meaning. Words are composed of one or more morphemes and are either the smallest units susceptible of independent use or consist of two or three such units combined under certain linking conditions, as with the loss of primary accent that distinguishes black·bird· from black·bird·. Words are usually separated by spaces in writing, and are distinguished phonologically, as by accent, in many languages.

Contents

Asomatous	13
Banausic	15
Cark	17
Decathect	18
Etiolate	20
Fantod	22
Graupel	24
Hypogeal	26
Immure	27
Jeremiad	28
Katzenjammer	30
Lacuna	32
Megrim	34
Nocent	36
Ort	38
Petrichor	39
Quader	40
Rimous	41
Somaticize	42
Tittle	44
Umbra	46
Ventifact	48
Wanchancy	49

Xerosere	51
Yare	52
Zoic	53

Words Some of Us Rarely Use

Asomatous[1]

To have it, be it
those mornings when you wake
and cannot turn your head.
The stiff column of your neck & spine
reminding you they exist & of how
limited peripheral vision is & more so
as we age, the eyes becoming nothing but
slits, wide-eyed wonder no more than a phrase.
This is when you wish for it &, too,
when winter comes ferocious, making its demands:
the coat, the gloves, the hat, the scarf, the boots,
the wariness of ice, the press of snow, the hands lying
chapped in your lap every evening.
    &, lastly, when hungry, that particular ache.

You see it as a flame, some carryover from those Sundays
when you accompanied your mother & served
as acolyte, good girl. The lit candle hovering
is what you wish to be. Only wind would frighten
or the wet pinch of fingers, nothing more. & not often.

The ease, the ease, & the weightlessness you try for those
days when you walk the house & gather items & drive a mile
to give them away!

---

[1] [ey-**soh**-muh-tuh s, uh-**soh**-] adjective 1. having no material body; incorporeal.

Sometimes, in certain settings, you near it:
the ascent into air, the descent into water, those
temporary states. But only sometimes & so briefly.

You dream of a room with one window & white walls,
a bed, a chair, a desk, three books, paper, pen,
the one painting no more than 8 X 8. & still too much
too often. You ask if three is too many, if the image
could rather, instead, be only recalled. If the words need
be written.

What is it you wish to cast off?
What more could you disown?

Banausic[2]

Certainly, the house you lived in. Something, yes,
that could be hauled up and hitched and transported.
Nothing of brick with cornices. Nothing
with a frieze, though you only learned that word later,
much later, in that art history course in the room that felt
as if it were underwater – the windows latticed,
the glass wavy, the light always dim.

Certainly, nearly everything in that house, too.
Unadorned table and chairs – easier to dust, to wipe clean.
Pattern-less coverlet with the straight edges. No scallop.
No embroidery to catch on
and snag.

And in each and every town and city, the post office.
Certainly, the one there, the one you drove to
with your mother when we wrote letters.
Stationed on the corner, windowless, to conserve, serve –
like the wood-burning stove in the basement
of your great-grandmother's farmhouse.

> That winter of the blizzard that forced us down
> into the cellars to keep warm.
> The clothesline strung to make our way from there

---

[2] [buh-**naw**-sik, -zik] adjective 1. serving utilitarian purposes only; mechanical; practical.

to there.

All this, so necessary. Sensible.
The trivet. The scratchy scarf of wool
that gave you a rash.

What we called: plain.
What we called: for use.

Cark[3]

Most often at night, before sleep, just after
the light has been turned off by someone else –
your mother, the girl paid to watch you until 11.

> What lay under the bed, waiting.
> Or behind the door, in that narrow space between.

Now, nothing as tangible as that.

Someone told you not to fret of anything more than three
months from now, and yet…
> there it is, looming. Nebulous.
> Like those Shakespearean ghosts in those mediocre
> film adaptations you were once made to watch.
> Or the fog over the bay that morning, the ferry
> making its wet hesitant way.

Ah, morning! How you long for it!

> What will serve to dissipate,   scatter.
>   A blind pulled up, clap
> of dawn leading to what can be seen
> or managed.

---

[3] [kahrk] noun 1. care or worry. verb (used with or without object) 2. to worry.

Decathect[4]

Tide in retreat, its recession from shore could be
what you envision once you close your eyes
and are asked what you see yourself as.
                                    That word
                        recession
chiefly of astronomy. What kind of moving away from
is that?

You sometimes picture that carnival ride – what some call
the Wave Swinger. The flinging out of
                            the long-chained seat.
No matter what is conjured.
It is what you do, sometimes
sooner rather than later.
But always, eventually. Loss being
what it is: a constant. A certainty. Death and taxes and loss –
what that poet wrote of so famously. The poem you read
when you were young enough to believe
everything on the page was true, was a guide, of sorts.
Not a manual, but nearly –
what you pointed to later and said, It's here, all here. *Proof.*
And, too, the father gone, each time farther – the postmarks
from states you'd never been. And then no more.

---

[4] [dee-kuh-**thekt**] verb (used with object) 1. to withdraw one's feelings of attachment from (a person, idea, or object), as in anticipation of a future loss.

You once asked her to tell you when you were doing it –
this verb – and within days it resembled nagging.

Now   and now   and now,
again.

As if you were born to it,
some sort of talent nurtured
and met with what you meant to protect
yourself from as confirmation.

Etiolate[5]

The coral bells pale on the west side
not from shortage of sun but too much;
noon and after blanches them, draining
all that drew you, their plum veins and leaves
speckled and mounded. What is this, then,
that speaks of lack of light? Both the second
and the third, here in this edition, and this one, too, though
the first makes no mention – only to be made sickly, absent
color and vigor. And this other text instructing full sun,
partial sun, though you know better, have seen
glare's damage:

        Up on the ladder, years before, in the interior
space, you brought the blue dress down to lay
in her arms. And you saw you were now
in possession of two blues as there are two
skies. Maybe even more. The spotlight's
hot bright gaze had done its work – drawing the eye
only to disappoint. You could not sell it even at half price,
could only with some craft you had not learned make two,
cutting at the side seams.

---

[5] [**ee**-tee-uh-leyt] verb (used with object) 1. to cause (a plant) to whiten or grow pale by excluding light: 2. to cause to become weakened or sickly; drain of color or vigor. 3. (of plants) to whiten or grow pale through lack of light.

Why not move what is sometimes called otherwise –
from the New Latin, that difficult word you must stop
and consider how to pronounce? You – who only somewhat
believe what others have to say. Why wouldn't you bring it
with its shallow roots up
and away from that constant roar and shimmer and bed it
in the cool shadow of the house?

Only east sun and only briefly.

Fantod[6]

Something like before
and during the exam,
all the word problems
in need of solving.
This house
on this lot shaped like so,
its perimeter this.
Or calculus with this
representing this, so then…

panic setting in.
The leg jigging,
the beads there,
above the upper lip.
Your eraser tearing the page
with the grubby work of it.

Later, a swell
and surge. The thrust
of chair
and withdrawal.

---

6 [**fan**-tod] noun 1. Usually, fantods. a state of extreme nervousness or restlessness; the willies; the fidgets 2. Sometimes, fantods. a sudden outpouring of anger, outrage, or a similar intense emotion.

This woman here
        and this man moving

                              out and away.

How fast,
the question.

Graupel[7]

Winter – the dreaded season.
The line of pines blocking the view,
and, always, the fumble
of mittens, like bandaged hands, and ice hidden
under the fresh coating of snow.
                          Months stretching out like years
as you ran those mornings
from the back door, open a crack –
just enough to hear and then see
the rumble and flash from down the road, to sprint down
the drive, that long black-topped drive, treacherous.

All the lights extinguished.
The hill you rode on your sled
the other day still showed the tracks
of your struggle to ascend, lay
with the sluggish river at its base. Was there
when you returned in the afternoon
and used the key hanging on a chain around your neck.
The house so cold you kept your coat on for an hour as you
listened to the ping of sleet hit the windows
and fretted and worried as if you were so much older
than you were.

---

[7] [**grou**-puh l] noun 1. snow pellets.

Once, you asked to go ice skating in town,
near the track, where they had flooded the field.
You pictured yourself gliding
in white skates, your hands snug in fur only
to be given a pair yellowed and broken, too big,
with a bunched sock in each toe, and no fur.
The blades of others gleamed, sharp, just missing
your fingers.

These, like bullets – these make sense
to you. Given those years.

Hypogeal[8]

Not so obviously, not so flagrant. No billboard.
No fishwife, calling from the back stoop. No parade
with its sequins and plumes and brash horns, the shine
        blinding.
Nothing of cacophony.

Subtle, subtle shifting. what may grow. Or not.

Even after that class, those books, you still stop
and ask: what rises from the floor, what descends
from the ceiling?

What extends unseen. The roots' sprawl.

Or burrows. The cicada nymph, differing
from what woke you in the summer months, as if the trees
were shrieking: that tymbal of the male, brash
for rutting.

Down, down in the muck of it. What lies in wait
for the heated moment, for day's end when you are tired
and yet another error has been made. And nothing
of emergence can be seen.

---

[8] [hahy-puh-**jee**-uh l, hip-uh-] adjective 1. underground; subterranean.

Immure[9]

Sometimes all or only partial, yellowed grin
sentinel, here.
Or the crumpled page
        or not, but flat, for warmth. Each, protection.

What we find.
This trinket once dangling from your wrist matters
more than that ship found in the earth, I say.
A grave, that. While this
of silver is talisman. Wear it now, wear it again
and see it shine and knock gently against the glass
you raise to your lips, with the fire ablaze.   Later,
we will set the stone here. Some will see it as that.
Others, my heart.

---

[9] [ih-**myoo r**] verb (used with object) 1. to enclose within walls. 2. to shut in; seclude or confine. 3. to imprison. 4. to build into or entomb in a wall. 5. Obsolete. to surround with walls; fortify.

Jeremiad[10]

In the long
hall
in the long
house,
there
we are
fixed
at two,
at five,
newly born,
almost
gone.
Mourn this:
the morning
of our long life.
And too:
you.
How you
would knock
at the carapace
we erected
in the noon
of our time.
How you

---

[10] [jer-uh-**mahy**-uh d, -ad] noun 1. prolonged lamentation or mournful complaint.

asked when
no one else
asked, wanting
to know of
that hall
and
that house
and
what we never had

to lose.

Katzenjammer[11]

The first definition, no. Or rather,
only three times, long ago
and far away, like that country of its origin
and yours. Or, most of yours – recall,
the grandmother from Prague.
    Ah,
he nods and smiles, hearing that.
As if you make sense now.

The second, yes. Often.
Though you do not keen. Do not wail. Have never
pulled your hair out.
Rather, mute queasiness, like motion sickness
without motion.
And the necessary food of the sick bed: dry toast
and sliced banana, an ice pop
not unlike the snow you used once
to cool your tongue – snow that had just fallen
and lay, thickening on the walk and lawn, that kept you

from the third – that riot. From
tapping into, yes, those bohemian ways
(And he nods some more.

---

[11] [**kat**-suh n-jam-er] noun 1. the discomfort and illness experienced as the aftereffects of excessive drinking; hangover. 2. uneasiness; anguish; distress. 3. uproar; clamor.

More fervently.) heard all the more
for the frozen ground,
because of the bare trees,
carried on the wind
that rattles the panes.

How odd, this word. For its assumed frolic and frisking.
Let's go to the katzenjammer tonight. Let's katz & jam.

But, no:
What comes after.
Or always.

Lacuna[12]

Argue without sense. Just the furor of the bee's sting
       and subsequent weeping.
       Quick anger and tears, the stopped
phrase, mid-sentence. *I do not want.* Or: *go ahead and.*

Tear the pages out in the middle
and near the end, where it gets interesting.

She walks offstage and doesn't return and we ask, *What
       became of her?*
Not even a few lines, like in Shakespeare, about her death.
Nothing.
Last you heard, she had moved to Texas
and wrote with sadness of the never-
ending flatness. Sure, there were sunsets, but.

Something's missing.

Way out on the peninsula, there was no service.
Even in the town, before the logging roads,
red and wet, nothing.
People used actual maps, folded in haphazard ways,
and tried not to think

---

[12] [luh-**kyoo**-nuh] noun 1. a gap or missing part, as in a manuscript, series, or logical argument; hiatus. 2. Anatomy. one of the numerous minute cavities in the substance of bone, supposed to contain nucleate cells. 3. Botany. an air space in the cellular tissue of plants.

of the movies they had seen or the books they had read
featuring disappearance,
absence, the answer
never given.

Megrim[13]

Begin with how it began – everything
slightly off:
        light on snow,
                      chatter in the hall.
        Brighter.   Harsher.
        Asking not to be looked at,
                heard.
Maybe the scent of something
you had not eaten, nor touched in years:
the clementine segmented.

Then, the snow was obliterated.
Bright shards winked and frisked.
The sides folded in and everything
narrowed and you thought of horses kept steady
on the trail. You had to turn to see,
if you wanted to see.

Those days, all you wanted
was a cool, dark room, muffled.
Your mother would knock on the door,
think you were lazy, moving into
those adolescent years. When all you really were
was waiting for something

---

[13] [**mee**-grim] noun 1. megrims, low spirits; the blues. 2. a whim or caprice. 3. migraine.

that would offer explanation.

Later, the pain did.
You dreamt of detaching your head
and setting it down
and picking it up later, much later.
Along the spine, in the shallow dips
at its tip, you pushed your fingers in
and knew momentary relief. Begged
for lovers in later years to press
until their hands ached, until something
like an ending could be seen.

Nocent[14]

Place this here.
        Put that there.
Say before thinking: *I never really*.
Walk away.

Assert that the tennis match you're scheduled to play
on this Saturday morning cannot be rescheduled
and though there may be a phone call that will bring her
to weeping, to recollections of that garden in another state,
a woman bending at the waist to pick a green bean and chew
on it thoughtfully, to hurried packing of something decent
in black, you need to go. Will go. Will be back later.

Not stemming from the archaic.
Rather adolescence and the paternal:
        You're just like your father.
Around the eyes and here. In this.
In: It's all about you.

What comes from him. That low-grade concern.
When you don't answer the email.
Don't attend the funeral because of your heart
condition. Nature. Nurture. Nature. Nurture.
And this just in the personal sphere. Imagine the larger.

---

[14] [**noh**-suh nt] adjective 1. harmful; injurious. 2. Archaic. guilty.

Whittle it down:
To do no harm.
 To do harm.

Ort[15]

The scrawl,
        the cheeky comment in ink on the glossy page,
and another, on the back of a photo. There on the shelf,
there in a box.
And the three-legged stool with its spinning top,   no
accompanying keys. There
in the corner.
And the white plates and bowls parceled,
stacked in the back of the cabinet.
One, two, and three.
One, two, and three.
And the skin of a berry
        or a fruit. Hanging limp on the tree,
lying, gutted, on the cutting board. Or
the bone.

---

[15] [awrt] noun 1. Usually, orts. a scrap or morsel of food left at a meal.

Petrichor[16]

The sandy clay found there and here is best.
And with what speed, the drop. Not one,
nor the other, but both, just so, just when.
Kizmet, she called it, standing in the house
you no longer own. Or fate. Or the ripening
for what beads and bursts and speaks
to another sense.
This and this, now.
And how we came here, accidently.
The turn that led to the valley
where the poppies are in bloom, swaying, swaying,
winking with their black eyes.
Or the mold on the plate, in the dish, blossoming.
Or the tree bark and coal tar, not to cure, but to color.
This and this, see.

This effervescence.
This union and scatter.

---

[16] [**pe**-trahy-kawr, -ker] noun 1. a distinctive scent, usually described as earthy, pleasant, or sweet, produced by rainfall on very dry ground.

Quader[17]

The shape drawn in the air. This, like so. All angles such, each side equidistant. Those corners sharp, the grim nub that always caught your knee. The bruise first a tender unseen & then not, taking its sweet time to yellow & fade. Those girls in their square houses with two stories & shutters, the front walk with the hearty flowers on either side. Those boys on the square, lying on their sides & propped up on their elbows. The compartment they're kept in is this & sometimes the square, the superscript that marks augmentation. When you recall. Or are reminded of. That maxim: measure twice, cut once. That footnote: plays well with. & yet: even this right margin is compromised, the ruler confirming. & so.

---

[17] [k dur] verb 1. to make something square 2. to agree with or get along with someone.

Rimous[18]

The mind, if we go that way. Or
the pine's bark, and what you saw from your perch
that summer.
The dried river bottom with the clay's color rising –
not Georgia's red, but northern – brown sugar packed down.
Grainy and rough. And never sweet, no.
        That summer so hot all was stasis – lying in bed,
lying under the willow, mustering something
to make your way to the platform in the pine's crook and sit
and listen to the tree creak and groan, it heave with wind
while the river bank crumbled.
        And now winter has its way with us
        and the maple-topped table. We take
        the beeswax and the cloth and form circles,
        that motion of sparklers, that shape we love
        best. To keep this at bay.
The mind folds in and you are there, back there, and there
will be no sparklers for fear of fire. And another word
surfaces – that of ridges found in leaves, not needles,
the pruned skin, the skin of the pudding your mother
skimmed off and said was just as good, just as worthy.
Offered as recompense.
The channel grows and widens and
        the spaces between.

---

[18] [**rahy**-mohs, rahy-**mohs**] adjective 1. full of crevices, chinks, or cracks.

Somaticize[19]

Who sleeps and dreams and does not want to wake
because of? They rise and fly or lie in sun or cross
paths with that one they have been waiting
all their lives to cross paths with. Not you.
For you, mornings are negotiation with yourself.
A reasoning that what you dreamt did not occur. No,
you have not perished, trapped in a car underwater. No,
the love of your life was not in the arms of another, smiling.
No, your teeth did not drop to the ground, one and two
and three and four.
But this process is difficult. You have lain in a mood
for hours, the sheets rucked around your thighs.
How are you to move forward?
You try for that song from that musical from that time
of angst, but it doesn't work. Has never worked. Has, in fact,
worked the opposite.
You fall back on the lives of others, who sleep and dream
and do not want to wake because their daytime lives
are something akin to horror. Doing so helps.
You are able to see the sense in thirty minutes on the bike
and brushing your teeth.
But all these dreams – the during and the after, the anxiety,
the wringing of hands, take their toll.
There's a dry cough.

---

[19] [suh-**mat**-uh-sahyz, **soh**-muh-tuh-] verb (used with object), somaticized, somaticizing. Psychiatry. 1. to convert (anxiety) into physical symptoms.

There's a pain there.
Your hair is thinning.
And all this furthers
the wringing of those hands.
And the dreams worsen.

Your grandfather died in his bed,
in his sleep, they said.
It must have been
his heart, they said.
But he had not seen three decades.
And no one confirmed.
What dream dreamt?

Tittle[20]

I don't give a rat's ass
first comes to mind. What your grandmother said.
Nights she smoked just her one cigarette and watched
Johnny Carson. This – the second definition.

Always second, with you. No, that's not true: once,
the blue ribbon for the crocheted pot holders.
The aluminum hooks that could gouge an eye,
if need be. Not that you ever.
And the ribbon, and the judge's comments: *First-rate work.*

First: this mark, here. Never quite above the I or the J,
those letters that came before yours.
Sometimes, not even. Sometimes entirely absent.
Some would search, mutter: *lazy* and *sloppy.*
Talk of Ps and Qs.

Or not. Rather: endear you to them. Wanting to fill
the space you evidently had missing, or had sloughed off.

And this: the third. Further explanation, like a footnote,
like what follows the semi-colon. And more – what is called
an *acute*, a *grave*, a *circumflex.*
What you open the additional tab for: to insert

---

[20] [**tit**-l] noun 1. a dot or other small mark in writing or printing, used as a diacritic, punctuation, etc. 2. a very small part or quantity; a particle, jot, or whit.

what is deemed *advanced*.

You were advanced for your age.
Though languages with these always tripped you up.
You learned your Spanish, only to switch to French,
and then be told your pronunciation was all wrong.
Not this way, but this way, the professor said.

The two of you stood in the classroom.
She'd say the word.
You'd say the word. In never quite the same way, watching
her lips move each time. Thinking of a speck
in the sky that must be a bird or a plane.

Umbra[21]

We mistake the one
for the other. Go in search of images
to aid with comprehension, trying,
sorting out the arrows, following
them to their end and noting
that this is the darker one,
the core, the deep center you said
in those years after you saw yourself as.
We were the moon, we suppose,
that astronomical body
both of us always gravitated more towards
than the sun, whoever that was.

We cannot help seeing
the eye in all of this.
Those instructional charts
hanging in the optometrist's office
while we wait patiently for a bright light
to temporarily blind us.
The pupil,
the iris,

---

21 [**uhm**-bruh] noun 1. shade; shadow. 2. the invariable or characteristic accompaniment or companion of a person or thing. 3. Astronomy. the complete or perfect shadow of an opaque body, as a planet, where the direct light from the source of illumination is completely cut off. Compare penumbra (def 1a). the dark central portion of a sunspot. Compare penumbra (def 1b). 4. a phantom or shadowy apparition, as of someone or something not physically present; ghost; spectral image.

the optic nerve extending out.
In one diagram, even, a candle is shown,
shining, its light projected through the lens
sitting behind the pupil, us.

We worry about going permanently blind,
the page with its script eroding, the spots
blotting out text, like the migraines we get
once a month. We think of Oedipus and Rochester,
Homer of that Greek world where shades played
their part, smudgy apparitions calling to us
as we stumble, unseeing. We fret about that kind
of blindness, though we perceive
we are already blind in other ways.

Ventifact[22]

To make, do. To make do. This, the last half, the word
within the word you know for certain – like we age
and gravity drops the ball, the stone into your hand.

All the stones in the bowl at the top of the stairs are smooth
not from wind but water. Or you suppose. Having been
picked from the beach, from the rocky jumble lakeside.

Not of desert, never having been – that landscape
he returned to. The tent pitched on the dune. The one
picture he sent that summer: *Where we are.*

And you thought: vista. And: expanse. And: this could be
that which draws you – the seam of sky and sand/water,
the wind ruffling up the edges only sometimes.

More: the clean line. The cleared space.

These other stones in the bowl to your right
are for caress – for soothing, of a kind, when nothing
comes, and wears you down, down. And sets you
in your place.

---

[22] [**ven**-tuh-fakt] noun, Geology. 1. a pebble or cobble that has been faceted, grooved, and polished by the erosive action of wind-driven sand.

Wanchancy[23]

Setting matters. What some call *context*.
The black cat, here. The opened umbrella, there.
And what – as in salt, as in mirror.
And who – as in you and you. You leaving to grieve,
to aid with grief. To serve as balm.
And you left in the house overlooking the lake, the A
of the house like that of the ladder, another of this.
Sad tale, this. Absent father & mother. Nothing of a sibling
anywhere. Ever. Just two people asking each other:
>   *What will stop her crying?* and
>   *Is the milk too cold, Is the water too hot?*

No wonder you wonder when, not if. Move quickly
to the second definition when someone seems to stick,
the surety seen as hazardous. As if,
>   as if any minute now,
>   > they won't be there.
>   > > > > Will go.

>   That term, *ghosting*.

And so, what if they stay?
Not leave the scrawl of directions –
>   *This much powder.*
>   *This spot, here, here on the wrist –*

---

[23] /wɒnˈtʃænsɪ/ adjective (Scot) 1. unlucky 2. dangerous; risky 3. uncanny; eerie.

but remain. Then, the third: all unsettles.
Prompts rising in the night to wander about, thinking
of unlatched doors,
of the shoes on the table,
of the purse on the floor.
It's an uneasy state, this.

Look at the word, you say. It's all there in the first
three letters: *pale* and *weak* and *strained* and *without
luster.*

Xerosere[24]

That mark there in the dry sand.

                                          Step off
from it and make another, and then start to take the rise
of the dune and see the scrubby grass there. And there.
Where not before.
Wind might do that – alter. More, other elements:
those wildfires that led you to email her, asking if
she had to go, packing hurriedly, the paint still wet
on the largest canvas, left.
Your eyes burned and stung, just thinking of it,
and you began to see them as an arid surface, too. Recalled
the scratch you got that one summer as a girl,
when you did what your mother said you shouldn't: rub
and rub, trying to alleviate. And all the while, a speck of glass
provoking some sort of change, though not good, not
positive, not going in the *right* direction. And certainly not
in what would be called a community, an *assemblage*.
Just your eye. Just you.
                        These thoughts you step off
from, that lead to this and this – the charred frame, salt
in the wound.   Remember:
the surface must be dry for this kind of succession.

---

[24] [**zeer**-uh-seer] noun, Ecology. 1. a sere occurring on dry soil.

Yare[25]

The gymnast's run & tumble.
The cricket. The acrobat. The life of every party.
The mother's grasp. The magician's hand. What comes
too soon
or not nearly soon enough.
The retort. Jack. The sailboat of wind & blade.
The squirrel's leap from branch   to branch,
from tree   to tree.
As if falling
wasn't an option.

---

25 [yair or especially for 1, 2, yahr] adjective 1. quick; agile; lively. 2. (of a ship) quick to the helm; easily handled or maneuvered. 3. Archaic. 1. ready; prepared 2. nimble; quick.

Zoic[26]

1. Not what has been etched – the equine, the canine, that feathered thing, but the thing itself. Having life, living first. The dog running in the long grass along the road, the horse keeping pace in the field near, or not. Rather, standing, its tail its only motion, that nonchalant gesture. The startled mourning dove rising with its screech something like the owl's – the owl seen more in stone than most anywhere else. Certainly not in the woods, in that tree he said one would be found. No, only once, in that large room, from his arm to hers.

2. If not the thing itself, its remains. The curled mollusk and soft-boned Aspidella defying permanence, saying, *Well why not me?* That which you examined in that other room with the cold fluorescent lighting, the tables with their tops of cold stone – another kind of. And failed at identifying, stunned by your ignorance, you who had collected agates and arrowheads and mica, sorting and storing and labeling with your childish script. To not know this, and so turn

to what was warm, what spoke with words.

---

[26] /ˈzəʊɪk/ adjective 1. relating to or having animal life 2. (geology) (of rocks, strata, etc) containing fossilized animals.

About the Author

Kelly R. Samuels lives in the Upper Midwest. Her poetry has been nominated for Best of the Net and has appeared in various journals including apt, *The Summerset Review, The Carolina Quarterly, Sweet Tree Review*, and *Split Rock Review*.

About the Press

Unsolicited Press started without the bootstraps in California in 2012, and has progressed to publish out-of-this-world fiction, creative nonfiction, and poetry. The team refuses to accept industry standards and acquires quirky, phenomenal, and true art from authors around the world. Learn more at www.unsolicitedpress.com.

www.ingramcontent.com/pod-product-compliance
Lightning Source LLC
Chambersburg PA
CBHW030134100526
44591CB00009B/653